S0-BNA-735

DISCARDED

Learning to Write
Expository Paragraphs

Frances Purslow

Weigl

CALGARY
www.weigl.com

Public Library

Incorporated 1862

Barrie Ontario

Published by Weigl Educational Publishers Limited
6325 10 Street SE
Calgary, Alberta, Canada T2H 2Z9

Website: www.weigl.com

©2009 WEIGL EDUCATIONAL PUBLISHERS LIMITED
All rights reserved. No part of this publication may be reproduced, stored in a retrieval system, or transmitted in any form or by any means, electronic, mechanical, photocopying, recording, or otherwise, without the prior written permission of the publisher.

All of the Internet URLs given in the book were valid at the time of publication. However, due to the dynamic nature of the Internet, some addresses may have changed, or sites may have ceased to exist since publication. While the author and publisher regret any inconvenience this may cause readers, no responsibility for any such changes can be accepted by either the author or the publisher.

Library and Archives Canada Cataloguing in Publication Data

Purslow, Frances
    Expository paragraphs / Frances Purslow.

ISBN 978-1-55388-436-1 (bound).--ISBN 978-1-55388-437-8 (pbk.)

    1. Exposition (Rhetoric)--Juvenile literature. 2. English language--Paragraphs--Juvenile literature. 3. Composition (Language arts)--Juvenile literature. I. Title.
PE1439.P875 2008   j808'.066   C2008-901428-6

Printed in the United States of America
1 2 3 4 5 6 7 8 9 0 12 11 10 09 08

Editor: Heather Kissock
Design: Terry Paulhus

Photograph Credits
Every reasonable effort has been made to trace ownership and to obtain permission to reprint copyright material. The publishers would be pleased to have any errors or omissions brought to their attention so that they may be corrected in subsequent printings.

Alamy: pages 9, 11L, 15, 17, 21L; **Canadian Museum of Civilization:** pages 4 (III-G-495, D20003-10543), 19L (VII-D-158, D2004-07196), 19R (III-F-213 a, b, D2004-22836); **Corbis:** pages 6, 7, 8, 11R (©Cedar Plank Partition, Canadian Museum of Civilization, v11-b-1527a-e, s94-6791), 16; **Getty Images:** pages 5, 12, 13, 14, 21R; **Library and Archives Canada:** page 21M (c-085137); **Nova Scotia Museum, Halifax:** page 10 (N-14,501).

We acknowledge the financial support of the Government of Canada through the Book Publishing Industry Development Program (BPIDP) for our publishing activities.

Table of Contents

What is an Expository Paragraph?

An expository paragraph is a group of sentences that explains or informs about a topic. There are many different kinds of expository paragraphs. One type explains how to make or do something. Another type presents a problem and possible solutions. An expository paragraph may also compare two or more people, places, or things.

The following is an example of an expository paragraph that explains Cree birchbark biting. If the steps are out of order in this type of expository paragraph, it is difficult for the reader to follow the process.

*Birchbark biting is a unique art form that has been practised by the Cree for hundreds of years. First, Cree artists trace a rough pattern on the back of a piece of birchbark and fold the bark into a small square or triangle. Then, the artists bite the piece of bark, following the rough patterns. The patterns form imprints on each of the sections of the folded bark. When the bark is opened, a **geometric** pattern emerges.*

Try making patterns by following the steps in the instructions. Substitute paper for the birchbark. Were the instructions easy to follow? Were all of the steps in the correct order? What would happen if the instructions were out of order?

Ordering the Steps

To make bannock, a **traditional Aboriginal** food, you will need special ingredients and equipment.

Ingredients
4 cups (1 litre) flour
1/2 teaspoon (2.5 millilitres) salt
5 teaspoons (25 mL) baking powder
1-1/2 cups (375 mL) water

Equipment
large bowl, measuring cups, wooden spoon, pan

There are many steps used in making bannock. Pretend you are telling a friend how to make bannock. What stages would be involved? For example, you might begin by mixing together the ingredients. What would come next? Use the pictures to guide you through the steps.

What are Pronouns?

An expository paragraph most often informs the reader about something or someone. The following example of an expository paragraph tells how useful birchbark was to the Ojibwa. In that paragraph, there are several pronouns. A pronoun is a word that takes the place of a **noun**. The pronouns are in red below.

*Birchbark was an especially useful material for the Woodland Ojibwa. It was used to build **wigwams**. Women used it to make birchbark bags and containers. Ojibwa men and women built birchbark canoes, too. These were strong enough to use on fast-flowing rivers. They were also light enough to carry between rivers and lakes.*

In the paragraph, the pronouns "it," "these," and "they" take the place of nouns. If the writer did not use pronouns, the nouns would have to be repeated. This would make the paragraph sound awkward and boring. Reread the sentence using the words "birchbark" instead of "it" and "canoes" in place of "these" and "they."

Learning to Use Pronouns

There are many types of pronouns. Personal pronouns stand for definite people, places, or things. "I," "me," "you," "he," "him," "she," "her," "it," "we," "us," "they," "them," "myself," "yourself," "ourselves," "itself," and "themselves" are examples of personal pronouns. Possessive pronouns show ownership. "His," "hers," "our," "ours," "my," "mine," "your," "yours," "their," and "theirs" are examples of possessive pronouns.

In the following expository paragraph, a dancer tells about dances performed at **powwows**.

Many different dances are performed at powwows. They all involve colourful outfits. I am a jingle dancer. My outfit is decorated with hundreds of small, metal cones. I perform with other jingle dancers. As we move to the beat of the drum, our outfits jingle to the beat. Another type of dance is the Grass Dance. It developed from an early warrior dance. A grass dancer's outfit has long pieces of yarn attached. As he weaves and steps, the yarn on his outfit sways like long pieces of grass. No matter which dance is being performed at the powwow, it is always danced in a circle.

Now read the paragraph again. Look for personal and possessive pronouns. Make a list of the pronouns you find.

Learning about Problems and Solutions

Another type of expository paragraph describes a problem and outlines possible solutions. The following paragraph explains a problem the Coast Salish encountered when building canoes. It also presents their solution to the problem.

The Salish needed canoes to fish at sea and to visit other villages. In order to build the canoe, they needed to fell a tree. Prior to European contact, the Salish did not have metal tools to cut down trees. Instead, they developed a unique way of bringing down a tree. They started by lighting a small fire at the tree's base. Feeding the fire with cedar bark chips hollowed the tree trunk until it burned right through and fell. The tree could then be carved and shaped into a canoe.

Can you identify the problem in this paragraph? What was the solution? Can you think of another way to fell a tree without using metal tools?

Practise Problem Solving

Read the expository paragraph about one of the difficulties of bison hunting and how the Blackfoot overcame this challenge.

Long ago, thousands of bison thundered across the Prairies. They were an important food source for the Blackfoot peoples living in the area. All Blackfoot groups smoked and dried bison meat. Each part of the bison had a special use.

The Blackfoot faced a big challenge when trying to hunt bison. These large animals were fast-moving and difficult to chase down. To solve this problem, the Blackfoot would chase the bison over cliffs. These cliffs were known as buffalo jumps, or pishkun. *In the mid-1700s, Europeans brought horses to North America. The Blackfoot could now keep up to the speed of the bison.*

Head-Smashed-In is one of the best-known buffalo jump sites in Canada. To learn about Head-Smashed-In, visit **www.head-smashed-in.com**. Why were the bison important to the Blackfoot? How did the way they hunted change after the arrival of Europeans?

Make a list of the problems the Blackfoot faced when hunting bison. For example, they needed to find a way to drive the bison over the cliffs. Next, make a list of the solutions. You might write that the Blackfoot shouted to frighten the animals.

Parts of an Expository Paragraph

An expository paragraph has three parts. The first part is the topic sentence. The topic sentence begins the expository paragraph. It presents the main idea of the paragraph. It tells readers what the paragraph will be about and catches their attention.

Supporting sentences follow the topic sentence. They provide details explaining or supporting the topic sentence. In this type of expository paragraph, the supporting sentences give the details of how two or more things compare to one another.

At the end of an expository paragraph, a sentence wraps up, or summarizes, the ideas expressed in the paragraph. This is called the concluding sentence. It is usually a strong statement.

Petroglyphs are a recorded history of Mi'kmaq life. They show how early Mi'kmaq saw their life around them. Some signs on a petroglyph have specific meanings. A triangle represents life-giving energy. Circles represent the Sun. Some Mi'kmaq petroglyphs are believed to be more than 2,000 years old. Today, Mi'kmaq petroglyphs can be found along the rocky shores of Canada's eastern provinces.

The topic sentence is shown in red in the paragraph. Can you tell which are the supporting and concluding sentences?

Identifying the Parts

Look at the photos. One shows a sculpture carved by an Inuit artist.
The other shows an example of Haida flat design.

Research more about these Aboriginal groups online and at the library. Write
a topic sentence for an expository paragraph about these different types of
Canadian Aboriginal artwork. Then, write two or three supporting sentences
comparing the two types of art. Finally, end your expository paragraph with
a strong concluding sentence.

Using Venn Diagrams

Before writing an expository paragraph comparing two or more things, a Venn diagram can be used to organize the information. Venn diagrams are a way of showing how things are the same and how they are different.

To create a Venn diagram, draw two overlapping circles. The part of the circles that is overlapping contains information that the two topics share. The parts of the circles that do not overlap contain information that is different for each of the topics.

For example, the Venn diagram below is about the traditional foods of the Ojibwa peoples. The overlapping centre of the circles shows foods the Woodland Ojibwa and the Plains Ojibwa had in common. The other parts of the circles contain foods that were part of the main diet for each group.

Woodlands Ojibwa   **Plains Ojibwa**

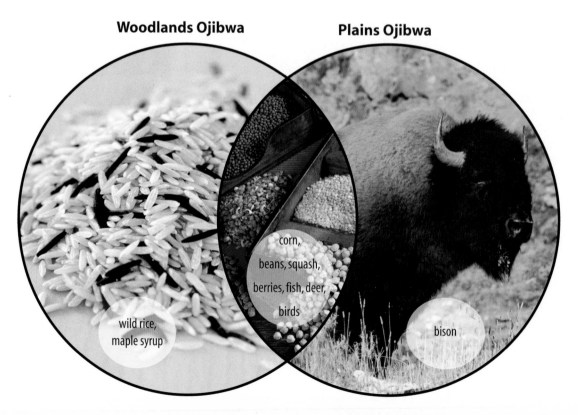

wild rice, maple syrup

corn, beans, squash, berries, fish, deer, birds

bison

Make Your Own Venn Diagram

Read the expository paragraph about two different types of Aboriginal powwows.

At powwows, Aboriginal dancers and drum groups perform in a large, circular area called an arena. There are two different types of powwows. There are competition powwows and traditional powwows. Dancers and drum groups compete for prize money at competition powwows. Dancers and drum groups do not compete at traditional powwows. Instead, they receive gifts.

What do these two types of powwow have in common? What are their differences? Make a Venn diagram using this paragraph. Now, look at the pictures of the powwow dancers. Write an expository paragraph by comparing what you see in the photos. Begin by making a Venn diagram. Then write a topic sentence, supporting sentences, and a concluding sentence.

Understanding Unity

All of the sentences in an expository paragraph should relate to the same topic. This is called unity. If a paragraph does not have unity, then one or more sentences do not relate to the main idea.

The following expository paragraph has unity. All of the sentences are about pemmican, a food made by the Métis and other Aboriginal groups.

For Métis living on the Prairies, bison was the main food source. It was often used to make pemmican. Pemmican was made from bison meat that had been dried in the sunlight. Once dried, the meat was pounded into a powder and mixed with bison fat and berries. The mixture was sewn into bags and stored. Pemmican was a staple in traditional Métis life as it could last for years and was easy to carry when travelling.

Which Sentence Does Not Belong?

The following paragraph does not have unity. It includes a sentence that does not relate to the main topic. Find the sentence that is out of place in this expository paragraph.

*The Denesuline used wigwams as their winter homes. To make a wigwam, the Denesuline built a dome-shaped frame that consisted of long, thin poles set into holes in the ground. First, each pole was paired with another. Each pair curved to form an arch that met at the top. The Denesuline are one of the largest **First Nations** groups living in the **subarctic**. Then, they tightly tied strips of animal hide to bind each pair together. Finally, several pairs of poles formed the dome frame.*

Go to **www.thecanadianencyclopedia.com**, and enter "Architectural History: Early First Nations" into the search engine to find out more about traditional Aboriginal homes. Use these facts to write your own expository paragraph about one type of home. Make sure that all of the sentences have unity.

Creating Coherence

The ideas in a paragraph should flow in a logical order from beginning to end. This is called coherence. Connecting words, such as "then," "next," and "finally," help show the order of time. These connecting words are called transitions. They connect the sentences and show the sequence of events.

Other transitions can be used to describe something in order of place, such as "nearby," "above," "inside," and "at the top."

The following expository paragraph has coherence. It explains how Iroquois women made pots in the past. Notice the transitions that show the order of time.

Iroquois women used special techniques to make pots. First, the potter ensured the clay was clean. Then, she added crushed rocks to harden the clay. Next, Iroquois women used their hands and simple tools to shape pots. While the clay was still damp, the potter pressed or scratched designs onto the surface of the clay. Then, the pots were placed in sunlight to dry. Afterwards, they were baked in a fire.

Put These Sentences in Order

This picture shows how Blackfoot women tanned bison hides. The hides were used to make **teepees**. Can you figure out the correct order of the sentences to create an expository paragraph with coherence? Look for clues to the correct order.

A. Then, the hides were washed and softened a second time.

B. Once dry, Blackfoot women rubbed animal fat and brains into the hides to make them soft.

C. First, the women stretched the hides and scraped them clean, using tools made from bones or elk antlers.

D. After stretching and cleaning, the hides were soaked in water for several days.

E. In the final step, the hides were smoked over a low fire to make them waterproof.

F. The hides were removed from the water and allowed to dry.

Answers: 1. C 2. D 3. F 4. B 5. A 6. E

Tools for Paragraph Writing

What did you learn? Look at the questions in the "Skills" column. Compare them to the page number in the "Page" column. Refresh your memory about the content you learned during this part of the paragraph writing process by reading the "Content" column below.

SKILLS		CONTENT	PAGE
Writing about how to do something		Cree birchbark biting, bannock	4–5
Using pronouns		birchbark uses, powwow dances	6–7
Writing about problems and solutions		Salish canoes, buffalo jumps	8–9
Understanding the parts of an expository paragraph		Mi'kmaq petroglyphs, Aboriginal artwork	10–11
Ensuring sentences have unity		Métis pemmican, Denesuline wigwams	14–15
Making sure the paragraph has coherence		Iroquois pottery, Blackfoot bison hides	16–17

Practise Writing Different Types of Sentences

Look at the photographs. One photo shows a Salish box drum. The other shows a Mi'kmaq handheld drum.

Use the Internet, or visit the library to find out more information about these types of musical instruments. Then, write four expository sentences comparing the two different types of drums. The four sentences should be a telling sentence, an asking sentence, an exclaiming sentence, and a commanding sentence.

In a telling sentence, the writer tells about something. This sentence ends with a period.

Asking sentences ask questions. They end with a question mark.

An exclaiming sentence shows emotion. It ends with an exclamation point.

Commanding sentences give direct orders. They end with a period.

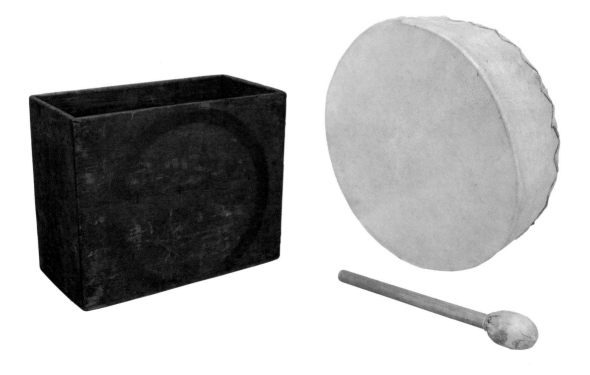

Put Your Knowledge to Use

Put your knowledge of expository paragraphs to use by writing your own paragraph. You could compare life for Canada's Aboriginal Peoples before and after Europeans arrived or show how Aboriginal Peoples did a task. You could also compare Aboriginal ways of life or show the problems they faced and solutions.

Read the following paragraph about the Inuit. It has a topic sentence, supporting sentences, and a concluding sentence. The sentences flow in a logical order and are related to each other.

The arrival of Europeans created many challenges for the Inuit. European settlers claimed and developed parts of the North. As a result, the Inuit lost control of their traditional hunting grounds. In 1999, the Canadian government divided the Northwest Territories and created a new territory called Nunavut. The Canadian government granted the Inuit control of 351,000 square kilometres of the new territory. The Canadian government remains active in Nunavut. It works closely with members of the Inuit community to ensure that Inuit concerns and traditions are addressed through the territory's own system of government.

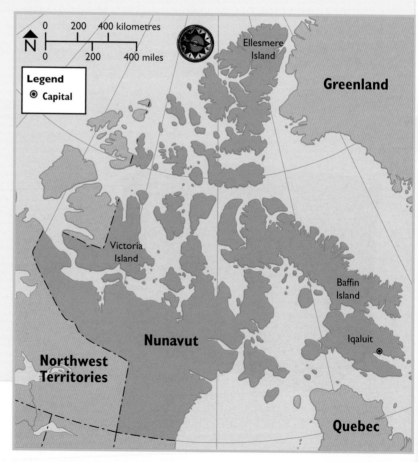

Choose one of the images below, and read its caption. Research the topic, and then write an expository paragraph. As you write your expository paragraph, make sure that it has a topic sentence, supporting sentences, and a concluding sentence. Choose only sentences that relate to your topic, and be sure that the ideas in your paragraph flow in a logical order from beginning to end.

In the early 1700s, a Denesuline woman named Thanadelthur helped the Hudson's Bay Company expand its trading area.

Hundreds of years ago, five North American Aboriginal nations came together to create the Iroquois Confederacy.

The first European contact with the Salish was made by Captain James Cook in 1778.

EXPANDED CHECKLIST

Reread your paragraph, and make sure that you have all of the following.

- ☑ My paragraph has a topic sentence.
- ☑ My paragraph has supporting sentences.
- ☑ My paragraph has a concluding sentence.
- ☑ All of the sentences in my paragraph relate to the same topic.
- ☑ All of the ideas in my paragraph flow in a logical order.
- ☑ I used pronouns in my paragraph to replace some nouns.

Types of Paragraphs

Now, you have learned the tools for writing expository paragraphs. You can use your knowledge of pronouns, problems and solutions, Venn diagrams, parts of a paragraph, unity, and coherence to write expository paragraphs. There are three other types of paragraphs. You can use some of the same tools you learned in this book to write all types of paragraphs. The chart below shows other types of paragraphs and their key features.

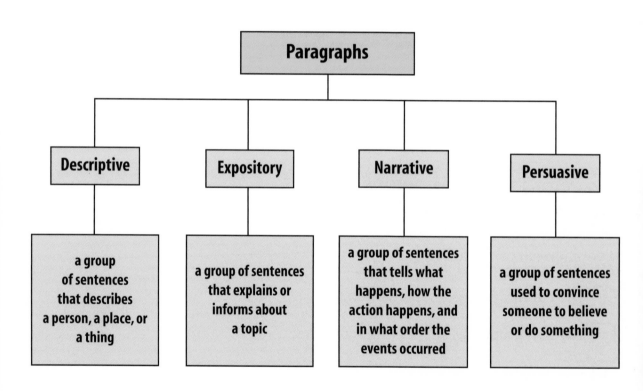

Paragraphs

Descriptive

a group of sentences that describes a person, a place, or a thing

Expository

a group of sentences that explains or informs about a topic

Narrative

a group of sentences that tells what happens, how the action happens, and in what order the events occurred

Persuasive

a group of sentences used to convince someone to believe or do something

Websites for Further Research

Books and websites provide information on writing expository paragraphs. To learn more about writing this type of paragraph, borrow books from the library, or surf the Internet.

To find out more about writing expository paragraphs, type key words, such as "writing paragraphs," into the search field of your Web browser. There are many sites that teach about Canada's Aboriginal Peoples. You can use these sites to practise writing expository paragraphs. Begin by selecting one topic from the site. Read about the topic, and then use the checklist on page 21 to write a paragraph.

Visit *The Canadian Museum of Civilization* to learn more about the first peoples to inhabit Canada, their culture, art, and ways of life.
www.civilization.ca/aborig/fp/fpint01e.html

Passageways provides information on historical events that impacted on Canada's Aboriginal Peoples.
www.collectionscanada.ca/2/3/h3-1110-e.html

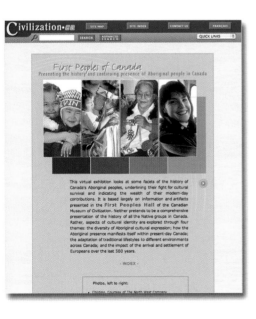

Glossary

Aboriginal: relating to an original inhabitant of a country

fell: to bring down

First Nations: members of Canada's Aboriginal communitiy who are not Inuit or Métis

geometric: featuring straight lines, circles, triangles, and other shapes

noun: a person, place, or thing

petroglyphs: rock carvings

powwows: Aboriginal events that feature traditional music, dancing, and singing

subarctic: a huge land region stretching across the upper part of northern Canada

teepees: structures made up of long poles set upright in a circle with hides or canvas stretched over top

traditional: long-established or passed down from parents to children

wigwams: structures made up of a cone-shaped frame that is covered with hides or bark

Index